LIFE CYCLES

Bumblebee

Ruth Thomson

WAYLAND

Explore the world with **Popcorn** - your complete first non-fiction library.

Look out for more titles in the **Popcorn** range. All books have the same format of simple text and awesome images. Text is carefully matched to the pictures to help readers to identify and understand key vocabulary.
www.waylandbooks.co.uk/popcorn

First published in 2009 by Wayland

Copyright © Wayland 2009

Wayland
Hachette Children's Books
338 Euston Road
London NW1 3BH

Wayland Australia
Level 17/207 Kent Street
Sydney NSW 2000

Managing Editor: Victoria Brooker
Concept designer: Paul Cherrill

British Library Cataloguing in Publication Data:
Thomson, Ruth
  Bumblebee. - (Popcorn: Life Cycles)
  I. Bumblebees - Life cycles - Juvenile literature
  I Title
  571.8'15799

ISBN: 978 07502 5785 5

Printed and bound in China

Wayland is a division of Hachette Children's Books, an Hachette UK Company.

www.hachettelivre.co.uk

Photographs:
Cover, 16, 22 (bottom right) Andrew Darrington/Alamy; 4/5 Anne-Marie Palmer/Alamy; 7 © Carl Morrow/ Alamy; 6 Dave King © Dorling Kindersley; 8, 22 Dietmar Nill/ naturepl.com; 9, 11, 19 © Scott Camazine/Alamy; 10, 22 John Mason/ ardea.com; 12, 13 John B Free/ naturepl.com; 14 Jerry Young © Dorling Kindersley; 15 © Redmond Durrell/ Alamy; 17 Kim Taylor and Jane Burton © Dorling Kindersley; 18 © Robert Llewellyn/Corbis; 20 Steve Hopkins/ ardea.com; 21, 22 Dr. John Brackenbury/ Science Photo Library

 Contents

Bees wake up

In early spring, a queen bumblebee wakes up from her long winter sleep.

She sucks sweet nectar and
eats pollen from flowers to
make her strong.

The queen bee

Like all insects, bumblebees have three parts to their body, six legs and two feelers.

two feelers for touching and smelling

large eyes

a pair of see-through wings

stripy, hairy body

The queen finds an empty mouse hole or bird's nest for her home. She makes a wax honey pot in her nest and fills this with honey.

An old bird's nest often has soft bedding for bees.

# Eggs

Next to her honey pot, the queen makes a ball of pollen and lays her eggs on it. She covers the eggs with wax.

The queen lays between four and ten eggs.

The queen sits on her eggs to keep them warm. She cannot leave them to feed outside, so she drinks from her honey pot.

 # Grubs

After about five days, the eggs hatch into white grubs. At first, they eat the ball of pollen.

The grubs have no eyes or legs.

Then the queen feeds the grubs
extra pollen and nectar.
The grubs eat and eat and
grow quickly.

 # Cocoon

Each fat grub spins a coat of silk
around itself. This is called
a cocoon. Inside it, the grub changes
into a bumblebee.

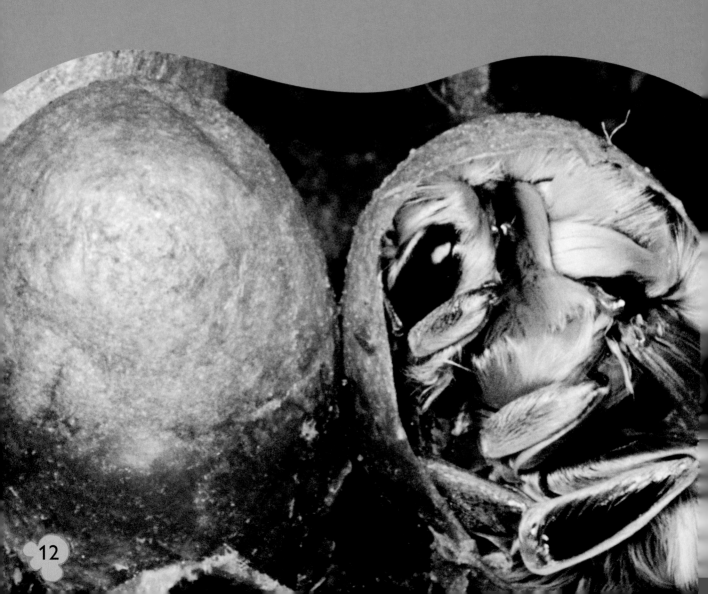

After two weeks, the bumblebees
are fully grown. They bite their
way out of the cocoon.

All new bees
are female.
They are called
worker bees.

Worker bees

At first, a worker bee is pale and damp. Its wings are soft. Soon its body becomes fluffy, its colour darkens and its wings harden.

Worker bees are smaller than the queen.

1 day

The queen lays more eggs.
The workers help the queen
to feed the new grubs.

Collecting food

The workers collect nectar from flowers as food. They carry the nectar in their stomach back to the nest. The nectar will change into honey to feed new grubs.

3 days

Bees suck up nectar through a long tongue.

The workers also collect pollen,
which they carry on their back legs.

Can you see
the pollen baskets
on this bee's legs?

A growing colony

The colony grows bigger and bigger.
By midsummer, there may be more
than 100 bees in the colony.

If the nest gets too hot, workers beat their wings very fast to fan air over it. This cools the nest.

Worker bees live for only a few weeks.

New queens and drones

In late summer, the queen lays male and female eggs. The male eggs hatch into drones. The female eggs hatch into new queens.

The young queens and drones leave the nest to mate.

The old queen, her workers and the drones die. The new queens burrow underground to sleep all winter. They will wake the following spring.

Bee life cycle

A queen bee lays eggs. The eggs hatch into grubs.
These turn into worker bees. Some of the eggs become
new queens or male drones, which leave the nest to mate.
After that, the new queens sleep all winter. All the other bees die.

eggs
In early spring, the queen
bee lays eggs.

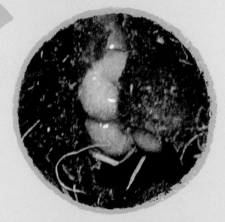

grub
An egg hatches into a fat grub
which spins a cocoon.

queen bee
The queen bee dies and a new
queen bee sleeps all winter.

worker bee
A worker bee comes out of the cocoon
and finds food to feed new grubs.

Make a bee mobile

Make a mobile of busy, buzzing bees to hang up.

You will need:

- yellow and black card
- scissors • cellophane
- pencil and black felt-tip pen
- sticky tape and glue
- wire coat hanger
- thread

1. Cut six oval shapes out of the card.

2. Draw black stripes and an eye on both sides.

3. Cut black card feelers and glue them to the head.

4. Cut cellophane wings. Tape one on each side of the bee's body.

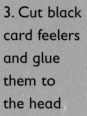

5. Tape a length of thread to each bee and tie the threads on to a wire hanger.

Glossary

colony a group of insects of the same type living together

drone male bees who do no work

grub the first young stage of many insects, including bees

hatch to break out of an egg

mate when a male and female come together
so they can produce young

nectar the sweet liquid inside many flowers that attracts insects

pollen the fine yellow powder in flowers

wax a sticky material made by bees

Index